Materialien für den bilingualen Unterricht
Geschichte

The American Revolution

A New Beginning

Cornelsen

Materialien für den bilingualen Unterricht: Geschichte
The American Revolution – A New Beginning

Erarbeitet von
Annegret Weeke, Düsseldorf

Didaktische Mitwirkung:
Manfred Wildhage, Braunschweig

Redaktion: Dr. Christine Keitz, Marc Proulx, Karsten Moß (Assistenz)
Karten und Grafik: Dr. Volkhard Binder, Berlin
Illustrationen: Gabriele Heinisch, Berlin; Thomas Binder, Magdeburg
Umschlaggestaltung: Klein & Halm Grafikdesign, Berlin
Layout und technische Umsetzung: werkstatt für gebrauchsgrafik, Berlin;
Heike Freund, Berlin

www.cornelsen.de

1. Auflage, 1. Druck 2007

Alle Drucke dieser Auflage sind inhaltlich unverändert
und können im Unterricht nebeneinander verwendet werden.

Druck: CS-Druck CornelsenStürtz, Berlin

ISBN 978-3-464-31042-7

Inhalt gedruckt auf säurefreiem Papier aus nachhaltiger Forstwirtschaft.

Preface

The American Revolution – A New Beginning is a bilingual module for use in your history class. Its units cover the important events before, during and directly after the American Revolutionary War. In this module you'll find the following elements:

Texts and Timelines
give you an overview of or introduce you to the subject. Words with an asterisk * are important history terms listed on the module revision page and explained in the Glossary of terms (see the Appendix, p. 22).

Sources
for your work: secondary sources, written primary sources, cartoons, portraits, statistics, photographs, maps and paintings. They are numbered throughout the module.

S 5 Tobacco exports from Virginia, 1616–1775 (in pounds)

Year	Tobacco exports
1616	2300
1617	20,000
1618	50,000
1622	60,000
1626	300,000
1639	1,500,000
1700	20,000,000
1775	100,000,000

History skills
introduce you to the work of historians. They give you strategies and tools for analysing the different kinds of sources.

Key terms and Biographies
These boxes give you further information on history terms or key personalities.

Biography

Thomas Jefferson

Jefferson – a lawyer and wealthy plantation owner – was born in Virginia in 1743. The "Declaration of Independence" from 1776 (S 14) was mostly written by him. His ideas of self-goverment and the natural rights of the people influenced the Declaration. In 1801 Jefferson became President of the United States and retired from office in 1808. He died in 1826.

New vocabulary
All numbered words[1] are explained or translated on the same page.

Tasks
In each section you'll find different kinds of tasks which help you to understand an event or development, for example
- by **organizing information** in charts and diagrams to simplify and summarize information, making it easier to understand and remember (see Appendix, p. 23).
- by **making connections:** tasks to critically question an historical interpretation, to draw comparisons or to relate historical events and developments to the present.
- by **doing extra research:** tasks that tell you to research a topic in a German history book, in an encyclopaedia, on the Internet, or in any other reference material. Present your results as a PowerPoint presentation or in any other form.

Activate your English
These boxes will help you to write and speak about historical topics.

Activate your English

Agreeing or disagreeing
In my opinion/view ...
I'm of the opinion that ...
I think it is right because ...
The source can serve as evidence because ...
I agree (very much) with the idea because ...
I disagree (entirely) because ...
I don't think so because...
I can't accept that because ...

Module revision
At the end of the module there are activities to revise key events, key terms and personalities, as well as history skills and vocabulary.

Appendix
The Appendix gives you a glossary of history terms, a glossary of biographies, an English-German vocabulary list, a historical dictionary and examples of the types of charts and diagrams used in ***The American Revolution – A New Beginning.***

The American Revolution – A New Beginning

1 The settlement[1] of North America

S1
Cornelius Wytfliet, Map of America, 1597

Native Americans

The first American immigrants, more than 20,000 years ago, were wanderers: hunters and their families following animal herds from Asia to North America, across a land bridge where the Bering Strait is today.

When Spain's Christopher Columbus discovered the New World in 1492, probably about 1.5 million Native Americans* lived in what is now the United States. Because he thought that the place where he landed – San Salvador in the Bahamas – was India, he called the Native Americans "Indians".

During the next 200 years, people from Europe followed Columbus across the Atlantic Ocean to explore America, set up trading posts[2] and found colonies[3] (see p. 10). Native Americans suffered[4] greatly when they came into contact with Europeans. Violent conflicts over land, along with alcohol and Old World diseases[5] to which Indians had no immunity, reduced their numbers to about 350,000 in the United States by 1920. Some tribes disappeared altogether. Today they number about two million (0.8 per cent of the total US population).

Many US place-names are Indian words, including the states of Massachusetts, Ohio, Michigan, Mississippi, Missouri and Idaho. Indians taught Europeans how to grow crops[6] that are now well known throughout the world, such as corn, tomatoes, potatoes and tobacco. Canoes, snowshoes and moccasins are among the Indians' many inventions.

1 settlement *Besiedlung*
2 trading post *Handelsstation*
3 found a colony *eine Kolonie gründen*
4 suffer *leiden*
5 disease *Krankheit*
6 crop *Feldfrucht*

European settlers[1] in North America

The English founded their first permanent colony* (Jamestown) in Chesapeake Bay in 1607. The French followed with their own colony, Quebec, in 1608, and soon after the Dutch began to settle in the region that became present-day New York. Within another generation, the Plymouth Company (1620), the Massachusetts Bay Company (1629), the Company of New France (1627), and the Dutch West India Company (1621) began to send thousands of colonists to North America: the French built up large territories along the Saint Lawrence River, the Dutch along the Hudson River, and the English in Virginia and Massachusetts.

Why did the settlers come?

Religious groups such as the Puritans* and the Quakers felt that they had to leave England because they were not allowed to practise their religion freely. The most famous group, the Pilgrim Fathers*, left Plymouth on board the *Mayflower* and arrived at Cape Cod Bay, Massachusetts, in November 1620. The hope of finding gold and treasure[2] attracted explorers and adventurers. Pamphlets[3] encouraged new emigrants and described America as a paradise. Thus Englishmen, Frenchmen, Germans, Scots, Irishmen, Dutchmen and Swedes crossed the Atlantic Ocean in search of rich, fertile[4] lands and a better life in the colonies.

Only a few colonists could finance their trip for themselves and their families to make a start in the New World. In many cases, their transportation was paid for by ship captains, merchants[5] and landowners who needed workers. In return, immigrants had to work as unpaid and unfree labourers[6] (called indentured servants*), usually for four to seven years. It has been estimated[7] that half the settlers living in the colonies south of New England came to America under this system.

S2 ***Nova Britannia: Offering most excellent fruites by Planting in Virginia,* by Robert Johnson, pamphlet, London 1609**

NOVA BRITANNIA.
OFFERING MOST
Excellent fruites by Planting in
VIRGINIA.
Exciting all ſuch as be well affected
to further the ſame.

LONDON
Printed for SAMVEL MACHAM, and are to be ſold at
his Shop in Pauls Church-yard, at the
Signe of the Bul-head.
1609.

1 settler *Siedler*
2 treasure *Schatz*
3 pamphlet *Broschüre, Prospekt, Streitschrift*
4 fertile *fruchtbar*
5 merchant *Kaufmann*
6 labourer *Arbeitskraft, Arbeiter*
7 estimate *schätzen*

S 3 William Bradford, author of *History of Plymouth Plantation*, 1630

William Bradford, one of the leaders of the group of Pilgrims known as the "Pilgrim Fathers", described their hopes and fears before sailing to the new land in his book History of Plymouth Plantation:

The place we had thoughts on were some of those vast and un-peopled countries of America. Although fertile, they are without civilized inhabitants. This idea [to go to those places] caused many doubts and fears among us. Some objected[1], saying that the length of the voyage[2] was such as the weak bodies of women and old people would never be able to endure[3]. And once there we should be in never ending danger of the savage[4] people, little different from wild beasts, who not only kill men, but torment[5] them in the most bloody manner[6] that may be imagined. We agreed that the dangers were great, but though they were likely, yet they were not certain. And all of them, through the help of God, by strength and patience, could be borne[7] and overcome.

William Bradford, History of Plymouth Plantation (1630), in: David D. Hall (ed.), Puritans in the New World, Princeton University Press, *2004, from: www.pupress.princeton.edu/chapters/s7738.html, 10 September 2005. Abridged and simplified by the author.*

1 **a** Photocopy the text on pp. 4–5 and underline all the important information on the settlement of North America (Who, what, where, when, why and how?).
b Draw a map of the North American continent. Then label[8] the map with lines, arrows and brief information on the settlement: e. g. draw a line to the place where Columbus landed. Label it with San Salvador. Note down the date of his landing.

2 In note form, write down information on the Pilgrim Fathers and the Puritans from the text on pp. 4–5 and from the Glossary, p. 26. Your notes should answer the questions: Who, what, where, when, why and how?

3 **a** Translate the title in S 2.
b Discuss the author's reasoning for writing the pamphlet. Who do you think he wrote it for?

4 **a** Find information on William Bradford (see S 3 and Appendix, p. 23), and organize the information in a mind map (see Appendix, p. 23).
b Note down in a bulleted list[9] the Pilgrim Fathers' hopes and fears before sailing to America (S 3).

5 Be a textbook author: Use the excerpt[10] from Bradford's account[11] (S 3) and write three sentences for a history textbook on the Pilgrim Fathers' view of the Indians in North America.

6 In US high school textbooks you may find sentences like: "The early European settlers expected to find an empty wilderness." Do you think Bradford's account (S 3) can serve as evidence[12] for this statement? Why or why not? Discuss in class (see **Activate your English**).

7 Organize the section "The settlement of North America" in an event map. For an example of an event map, see Appendix, p. 23.

8 **Extra research:** Give a PowerPoint presentation on Christopher Columbus (see S 1, the person in the top left-hand corner).

Activate your English

Agreeing or disagreeing
In my opinion/view ...
I'm of the opinion that ...
I think it is right because ...
The source can serve as evidence because ...
I agree (very much) with the idea because ...
I disagree (entirely) because ...
I don't think so because...
I can't accept that because ...

1 object to sth. *einwenden*
2 voyage *journey, trip*
3 endure sth. *etwas ertragen*
4 savage *wild*
5 torment sb. *jdn. quälen, foltern*
6 manner *way*
7 bear – bore – borne sth. *etwas ertragen*
8 label *beschriften, kennzeichnen*
9 bulleted list *Aufzählung (mit Aufzählungszeichen am Zeilenanfang)*
10 excerpt *Ausschnitt*
11 account *Bericht*
12 evidence *Beleg, Beweis*

2 Involuntary[1] immigrants

Shiploads of unfree labourers

The first black Africans were brought to Virginia in 1619, just 12 years after the founding of Jamestown. In the beginning, many were seen as "servants"[2] who could earn their freedom just like the white indentured servants*. In 1664, however, the colony of Maryland declared that all blacks and their children in the colony would "serve for life". Virginia soon followed the example. From then on, more and more black slaves[3] worked on the booming tobacco plantations[4] in Virginia and Maryland instead of white indentured servants. Although some slaves lived as household servants in the Middle Atlantic and New England colonies, the majority of slaves worked on the cotton[5] and rice plantations in the southern colonies of Virginia, Maryland, South Carolina and Georgia.

S4 **A tobacco plantation on the title page for the 1788 commentary of the US Constitution**

S5 **Tobacco exports from Virginia, 1616–1775 (in pounds)**

Year	Tobacco exports
1616	2300
1617	20,000
1618	50,000
1622	60,000
1626	300,000
1639	1,500,000
1700	20,000,000
1775	100,000,000

S6 **Slave population of Virginia, 1619–1860**

Year	Number of slaves	Number of total population	Percentage of enslaved
1619	20	1000	2.0
1625	23	1232	1.8
1648	300	15,000	2.0
1670	2000	40,000	5.0
1700	8000	58,000	13.7
1750	120,000	231,000	51.9
1800	339,796	807,557	42.1
1820	411,886	938,261	43.9
1840	431,873	1,025,227	42.1
1860	472,494	1,219,630	38.7

S 5, S 6: www.slaveryinamerica.org/history/hs_es_tobacco_slavery.htm; www.economics.ucr.edu/papers/papers03/03-12.pdf; www.eh.net/encyclopedia/?article=wahl.slavery.us, 10 September 2005.

9 Explain the difference between indentured servants and slaves (see the text).

10 **a** Present the development of the number of slaves (S 6) and of the tobacco exports from Virginia (S 5) in two line graphs.

b Write a paragraph describing the development of the number of slaves in S 6.

11 **a** Describe the development of tobacco exports from Virginia in the 17th and 18th centuries (S 5).

b Compare the growth of the tobacco exports (S 5) with the development of slavery (S 6) and draw conclusions[6].

Activate your English

Talking about statistics

Figures increased[7] / rose / went up ...
There was an increase / a rise in ...
Figures decreased/dropped/fell ...
There was a decrease/drop/fall in ...
Figures remained steady ...
to rise sharply/dramatically/slightly/gradually
to rise by ... per cent / by 100,000

1 involuntary *unfreiwillig*
2 servant *Diener*
3 slave *Sklave (see also Appendix, p. 22, "slave trade")*
4 plantation *Plantage; landwirtschaftlicher Großbetrieb in warmem Klima, der sich auf die Erzeugung eines Produktes spezialisiert*
5 cotton *Baumwolle*
6 draw conclusions *Schlüsse ziehen*
7 increase *steigen, (an)wachsen*

Evaluating sources

Primary sources versus secondary sources

Historians use primary sources[1] to get as close as possible to what actually happened during an historical event or time period. William Bradford's description of the Pilgrims' hopes and fears[2] (S 3, p. 6) is an example of a primary source. However, historians also use secondary sources[3]. For example, the text on p. 6 is a secondary source. Every historian who writes a textbook uses primary sources as well as secondary sources.

What is the difference?

In the simplest sense, primary sources are texts or other materials produced during the time in history which you are studying.
Secondary sources are materials
– produced by people in a later period;
– which use primary sources as evidence and examples;
– which often express an opinion or an argument about a past event or time period.
Magazine articles from December 1989, for example, are primary sources for the study of the German unification[4] in 1989–1990. But any book or magazine article or movie published or released much later about the unification is a secondary source.

S2 *Nova Britannia: Offering most excellent fruites by Planting in Virginia*, by Robert Johnson, London 1609

S5 Tobacco exports from Virginia, 1616–1775 (in pounds)

Year	Tobacco exports
1616	2300
1617	20,000
1618	50,000
1622	60,000
1626	300,000
1639	1,500,000
1700	20,000,000
1775	100,000,000

S8 Colonies in North America, 1750

Study skills

Primary sources

1. Personal records[5] or documents: diaries, journals, letters, manuscripts, speeches
2. Autobiographies and memoirs[6]
3. Government documents and records, laws, census[7] statistics, treaties[8]
4. Court records
5. Business records and contracts[9]
6. Published materials: books, magazines, newspaper articles, reports written at the time
7. Novels, dramas written at the time
8. Visual materials: photographs, paintings, sculptures, films, video recordings, cartoons
9. Audio materials: radio broadcasts
10. Physical objects from that time: clothes, furniture, toys, buildings

Secondary sources

1. Articles and books on historical topics
2. Reference material such as encyclopaedias
3. Documentary films on historical topics
4. Biographies

1 primary source *Primärquelle*
2 fear *Angst*
3 secondary source *Sekundärquelle, Sekundärtext*
4 unification *Vereinigung*
5 record *Aufzeichnung*
6 memoir *Lebenserinnerung*
7 census *Volkszählung*
8 treaty *Vertrag zwischen Staaten*
9 contract *geschäftlicher Vertrag*

What can you learn from primary and secondary sources?

Many pupils expect to learn from their history textbook about the past "as it really happened". Historians writing textbooks today agree, however, that it is impossible to know what exactly happened in history, as nobody can say exactly what happened last week in their family, in their city, in their country, or anywhere in the world.

A history textbook is written by authors who have examined a subject, have studied primary and secondary sources, and have drawn certain conclusions. Of course, different authors draw different conclusions and interpret their sources differently.

Primary sources like letters, reports of an event, diaries, etc. also contain personal interpretations of what happened. Every document has a creator, and every creator has a point of view, blind spots[1] and biases[2]. Remember that just because something was published does not make it truthful, accurate or reliable[3].

S 7 Examples of primary and secondary sources

Primary source	Secondary source
Painting: Johannes A. S. Oertel, "New Yorkers pull down a statue of King George III on 9 July 1776" *p. 13*	Article in school textbook analysing the painting
Letter from Thomas Jefferson	Biography of Thomas Jefferson
A poem about slavery	Essay on poetry in the 18th century
Statistics on the slave population in 17th-century Virginia *p. 7*	Article about slave trade in an encyclopaedia
Political cartoon: "The Horse 'America', Throwing His Master" *p. 17*	Book about the American War of Independence

S 13 **Johannes A. S. Oertel (1823–1909), New Yorkers pull down a statue of King George III on 9 July 1776, painting, c. 1859.** *The event took place after news of the Declaration of Independence.*

S 9 The historian Alan Taylor writes about the white colonial population, 2003

During the seventeenth century, New England (New Hampshire, Massachusetts, Connecticut, Rhode Island) received only 21,000 emigrants – very few compared to the 120,000 transported to the Chesapeake Bay area (Virginia, Maryland) or the 190,000 who colonized the West Indies (St. Kitts, Barbados, Bermuda, Nevis).

S 17 The US Constitution

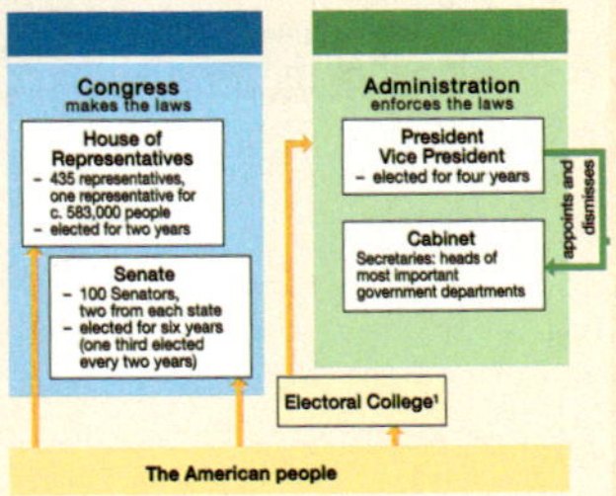

12 **a** Look at the primary sources listed in S 7: find out their dates of creation and put the primary sources in chronological order.

b Make a three-column chart like in S 7: fill in the primary sources used so far in Units 1 and 2. Then note down where these primary sources could be used (in which kind of secondary source).

13 Bias in primary sources: Many immigrants wrote letters to their families in Europe describing their new life in America. Are these letters good primary sources on life in America at a certain time? List the arguments for and against their use in a two-column chart.

14 **Extra research:** In class, choose an object (somebody's pencil case, mp3 player, maths exercise book, etc.). Imagine this object as a primary source in an exhibition[4] in 2100 about life in Germany at the beginning of the 21st century. Write a short text for the exhibition describing and explaining this object (its use, owner, design, etc.).

1 have blind spots *„auf einem Auge blind sein", bestimmte Dinge nicht wahrnehmen*
2 bias *Tendenz, Voreingenommenheit, Neigung*
3 reliable *verlässlich*
4 exhibition *Ausstellung*

3 The colonies

Who rules[1] in the colonies?

The royal government in London ruled its colonies through royal governors. But in North America, all free men had a say in government[2]. They elected representatives[3] to a parliament (assembly[4]) which had the right, for example, to vote on[5] taxes for their colony. Yet[6] free women had no right to vote.

The distance between England and its colonies made control of them difficult, and the colonies practically governed themselves.

S 8 **Colonies in North America, 1750**

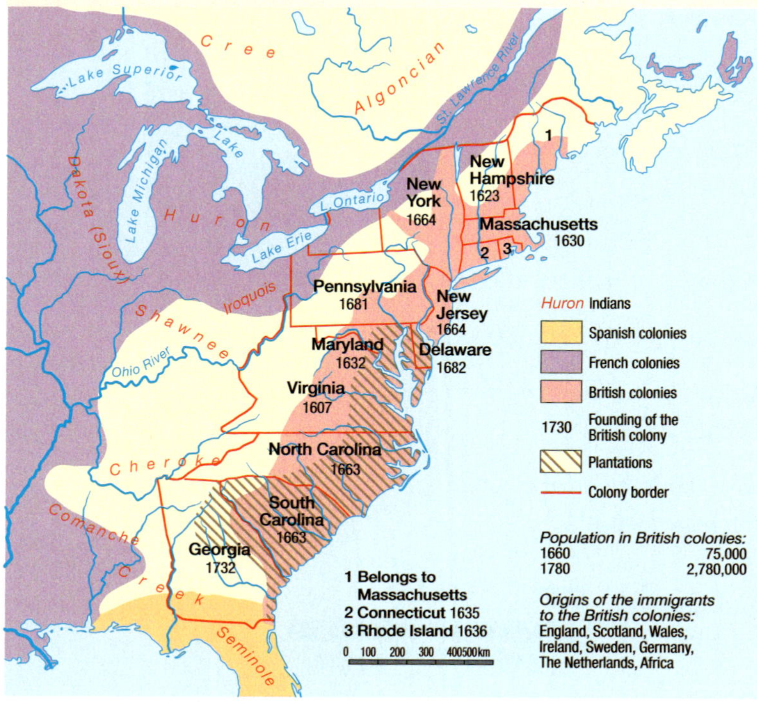

S 9 **The historian Alan Taylor writes about the white colonial population, 2003**

During the seventeenth century, New England (New Hampshire, Massachusetts, Connecticut, Rhode Island) received only 21,000 emigrants – very few compared to the 120,000 transported to the Chesapeake Bay area (Virginia, Maryland) or the 190,000 who colonized the West Indies (St. Kitts, Barbados, Bermuda, Nevis).
Yet in 1700 New England's population had grown to 91,000, while only 85,000 whites lived in the Chesapeake Bay area and 33,000 in the West Indies.

Alan Taylor, "The People of British America, 1700–1750" (2003), from: www.fpri.org/orbis/4702/taylor.peoplebritishamerica1700.html, 20 September 2005. Simplified by the author.

15 **a** Read the text and start an English-German vocabulary list "Political terms and phrases".
b "The political system of the colonies was democratic." Do you agree with this statement? Give reasons for your opinion (see **Activate your English**, p. 6).

16 **Extra research:** Photocopy the map in S 8. Compare it with a present-day map of the United States and label your copy with the most important cities in the former colonies.

17 **a** Compare the distances between the cities (see Task 16) with the distances between your hometown and some cities in Europe.
b Speculate on how the distances affected life in the colonies.

18 **a** Organize the information (given by Taylor) in S 9 in a table like the one below.
b Speculate about possible reasons for the differences. Vocabulary help: *White people might/could have …*

Colonies	*Arrival of white emigrants during the 17th century*	*White population in 1700*
…	…	…

1 rule *herrschen*
2 have a say in government *ein Mitspracherecht in der Regierung haben*
3 representative *Abgeordneter*
4 assembly *Versammlung*
5 vote on sth. *über etwas abstimmen*
6 yet *jedoch, aber*

4 From resistance[1] to open rebellion (1763–1776)

1763: The turning point in American colonial history?

By the mid-1700s, Britain and France were bitter rivals for colonies in the Caribbean islands and on the North American continent. From 1756 to 1763 they fought the Seven Years War both in Europe and in America. At the end of the war, when the British army captured[2] Montreal and Quebec in "New France", the dream of a French empire[3] in North America was over. In 1763, the Peace Treaty of Paris gave all the lands between the Atlantic Ocean and the Mississippi River to the British.

The conflict between Britain and its American colonists began in 1763. In this year Parliament in London passed a law[4] to raise money[5] for its 10,000 troops in the colonies through a Stamp Tax. Colonists had to pay a tax on every piece of printed paper: ship's papers, legal documents, licenses, newspapers and even playing cards were taxed. A stamp on the pieces of paper showed that the tax had been paid. The colonists protested at once. Parliament had no right to tax them, they argued, since they elected no members of the Parliament in London.

The build-up[6] to revolution – A timeline

The following timeline shows how resistance* against the sugar tax in 1764 turned into an open rebellion against the British King in 1776:

1764 **Sugar Act** increases tax on all sugar; angry reactions, threat[7] of a boycott of English products.

1765 **Stamp Act** results in widespread opposition: meeting of delegates[8] from the different colonies in New York under the slogan "No taxation without representation"; protest meetings; attacks against stamp masters; boycott of British goods; riots[9].

1766 **Stamp Act** repealed[10].

1767 **Townshend Duty Act** imposes taxes[11] on paper, glass and tea imported from England. Boycott of British imports.

1768 Customs officers[12] are attacked by a mob in Boston; rioting against British property[13]; British troops are stationed in Boston.

1770 **Townshend Duty Act** repealed (except tea).

1773 **Tea Act** excludes[14] colonial merchants and ship owners from the profitable tea trade[15]. Public anger[16] forces British ships full of tea to return to England. "Boston Tea Party": In December, colonists dressed as Indians throw tea into the water to protest against the tax on tea.

1774 **Coercive Acts** (called "Intolerable Acts" in America) close the port in Boston and give more power to the royal governors.

September/October: Representatives from all the colonies (except Georgia) attend the **First Continental Congress** and protest against the acts. The Congress votes to stop all trade with Great Britain until Parliament repeals the "Intolerable Acts".

1775 In New England men begin arming themselves.

April: The British commander in Boston sends soldiers to Concord (near Boston) to find illegal guns and munitions. At Lexington Green, the British are attacked by 70 armed Massachusetts militiamen[17] (Minutemen). The first shots kill eight and wound ten Americans.

August: King George III declares that the colonists stand in open rebellion to his authority and that the "rebels" in the colonies will be hung as traitors[18].

S 10 British government stamp showing that a tax has been paid, 1765

French text on the stamp: "Ho(n)ni soit qui mal y pense" (Ein Schuft, wer Böses dabei denkt).

1 resistance *Widerstand*
2 capture sth. *etwas einnehmen*
3 empire *Reich*
4 pass a law *ein Gesetz verabschieden*
5 raise money *Gelder aufbringen*
6 build-up *Aufbau*
7 threat *Drohung*
8 delegate *Abgeordneter, Beauftragter*
9 riot *Aufruhr, Krawall*
10 repeal (a law) *(ein Gesetz) aufheben, abschaffen*
11 impose taxes *Steuern auferlegen*
12 customs officers *Zollbeamte*
13 property *Besitz*
14 exclude sb. *jdn. ausschließen*
15 trade *Handel*
16 anger *Wut, Zorn*
17 militia *Bürgerwehr, Miliz*
18 traitor *Verräter*

1776 January: Thomas Paine publishes bestselling pamphlet[1] *Common Sense* (120,000 copies are sold in three months). In it, he speaks openly of "independence" from Britain and of a government in which the people rule through their elected representatives.

4 July: Declaration of Independence[2]. Representatives of the thirteen colonies of North America, meeting for the Second Continental Congress since May 1775, declare their separation, freedom and independence from the United Kingdom of Great Britain.

1 pamphlet *Streitschrift*
2 Declaration of Independence *Unabhängigkeitserklärung*
3 disobedience *Ungehorsam*
4 injustice/unjust *Ungerechtigkeit/ungerecht* justice/just *Gerechtigkeit/gerecht*
5 refusal *Weigerung*
6 insurrection *Aufruhr, Aufstand, Erhebung*
7 suicide *Selbstmord*
8 aim *Ziel, Absicht*
9 dismissal *Entlassung*
10 abdication *Abdankung*
11 overthrow *Umsturz (einer Regierung)*
12 investigation *Untersuchung*
13 act *a law that has been passed by a parliament*
14 engraving *Stich, Druckgrafik*

Forms of resistance

When governments make unpopular laws or take actions which are highly unpopular, people openly show their resistance*. Protest, disobedience[3] or resistance can take many different forms:
- verbal protests (public debates, songs, etc.);
- written or printed protests to bring wider attention to the injustice[4] (political cartoons, pamphlets, etc.);
- refusal[5] to follow instructions or laws;
- economic protests (strikes, etc.);
- armed/violent resistance (mob riots, insurrections[6], civil war, etc.).

Other non-violent and violent examples of 21st-century resistance are: sit-ins, hunger strikes, street demonstrations, letters to the editor, kidnappings, suicide[7] bombings.
The aim[8] and result of resistance can be: the repeal of a law, reforms, the dismissal[9] of a minister, the abdication[10] of a monarch, the overthrow[11] of a government, independence.
Use the following questions to structure your investigation[12] of resistance down through history: What do people do to resist? What is the aim of the protest actions? What do people risk by resisting?

S 11 Daniel Chodowiecki (1726–1801), Resistance to the Stamp Act of 1765[13], engraving[14], Germany, 18th century

An angry Boston crowd burns a pile of stamps in resistance to the Stamp Act of 1765. Note that the artist included women and an African-American among the protesters.

S 12 Daniel Chodowiecki (1726–1801), The Boston Tea Party on 16 December 1773, engraving, Germany, 18th century

Colonists dressed as Indians throw tea into Boston Harbour to protest the tax on tea.

S 13 Johannes A. S. Oertel (1823–1909), New Yorkers pull down a statue of King George III on 9 July 1776, painting, c 1859

The event took place after the news of the Declaration of Independence had reached New York. Vocabulary help: a crowd of people – cheer sb. on – a rope is slung around – iron bars – wooden poles – smash to pieces – pedestal[1]

19 Read the text "Forms of resistance" on p. 12. Give a current example of an unpopular law or a government action and people's resistance to it.

20 Look at the timeline on pp. 11–12 and the visual sources S 11–S 13:

- **a** Write down American colonists' demands in their protest meetings.
- **b** Note down the causes of the colonist's protests.
- **c** List the forms of the colonists' resistance to the laws of the British government and match them with those listed in the text "Forms of resistance".
- **d** Place the forms of resistance in order from least violent to most violent.
- **e** Describe how the British reacted to the complaints[2], demands and acts of violence.
- **f** Discuss whether, in your opinion, the reactions were justified[3].

21 Copy the chart below and list people, objects and activities in S 13. For unknown terms and phrases, check the Historical dictionary (p. 26) or a German-English dictionary.

22 Write a newspaper article for the *London Illustrated News* about the events in New York on 9 July 1776. Speculate about people's motives.

people	*objects*	*activities*
...	...	...

1 pedestal *Sockel, Unterbau*

2 complaint *Beschwerde*

3 justify *rechtfertigen*

5 Winning independence

The American Revolutionary War (1775–1783)

The American Revolutionary War, also called the American War of Independence, lasted[1] from 1775 to 1783. It ended two centuries of British rule for most of the North American colonies and created the new United States of America.

The "shot heard round the world" fired at Lexington on 19 April 1775 (see timeline, pp. 11–12) began the war, and the Peace Treaty of Paris ended it eight and a half years later on 3 September 1783.

General George Washington (see Biography, p. 18) commanded the American army of 20,000 poorly paid and trained militiamen. 42,000 professional soldiers fought in the British army, along with 30,000 troops which the British government had bought from a number of German princes[2]. It seemed completely impossible that the "rebel army" could defeat the British. But General Washington proved to be a fine commander, and took advantage of the mistakes of the British generals. In 1778 Major General Baron von Steuben, who had been an officer in the Prussian[3] army, began training the American regiments. Slowly he turned them into a more powerful army.

Without French help, however, the colonists could not have defeated Britain's troops. France secretly gave supplies[4] and money to the colonies from 1776 to 1778. After declaring war on England in June 1778, the French government also sent soldiers and ships.

In the Treaty of Paris (1783), Great Britain formally recognized[5] the thirteen colonies as the United States of America.

Biography

Thomas Jefferson

Jefferson, a lawyer and wealthy plantation owner, was born in Virginia in 1743. The Declaration of Independence of 1776 (S 14) was written mostly by him. His ideas on self-government and the natural rights of the people greatly influenced the Declaration. In 1801, Jefferson became President of the United States and served until 1808. He died in 1826.

S 14 Extracts from the Declaration of Independence, 4 July 1776

English version	*German translation*
(1) When in the course of human events, it becomes necessary for one people to dissolve the political bands which have connected them with another [...], a decent respect to the opinions of mankind requires that they should declare the causes which impel them to the separation.	Wenn es im Laufe von geschichtlichen Ereignissen für ein Volk notwendig wird, die politischen Bande aufzulösen, die es bisher mit einem anderen vereinten [...], so erfordert die geziemende Achtung vor der Meinung der Welt, dass es die Gründe angibt, die es zur Trennung zwingen.
(2) We hold these truths to be self-evident, that all men are created equal; that they are endowed by their creator with certain unalienable rights, that among these are life, liberty and the pursuit of happiness; that to	Wir halten diese Wahrheiten für selbstverständlich, dass alle Menschen gleich geschaffen worden sind; dass sie von ihrem Schöpfer mit bestimmten unveräußerlichen Rechten ausgestattet sind, zu denen Leben,

1 last *dauern*
2 prince *Fürst*
3 Prussian/Prussia *preußisch/Preußen*
4 supply *here: munitions, arms, food, etc (Nachschub)*
5 recognize sth. *etwas anerkennen.*

secure these rights, governments are instituted among men, deriving their just powers from the consent of the governed; that whenever any form of government becomes destructive of these ends, it is the right of the people to alter or to abolish it, and to institute a new Government [...].

(3) The history of the present King of Great Britain [...] is a history [...] of an absolute tyranny[1] over these [colonies]. [He made it hard for parliaments to meet. He tried to abolish[2] parliaments. He kept armies in the country without the people's consent[3]. He introduced taxes without the people's consent. He began a war against Americans.] [...]

(4) We, therefore, the representatives of the United States of America [...] do, in the name [...] of the good people of these colonies, [...] declare, that these united colonies are [...] free and independent States [...], and that all political connection between them and the State of Great Britain, is [...] totally dissolved. [...]

Freiheit und Streben nach Glück gehören; dass zur Sicherung dieser Rechte Regierungen unter den Menschen eingesetzt sind, die ihre rechtmäßige Gewalt von der Zustimmung der Regierten herleiten; dass, wenn immer eine Regierungsform diesen Zielen schadet, es das Recht des Volkes ist, sie zu ändern oder abzuschaffen und eine neue Regierung einzusetzen [...].

English version: www.ushistory.org/declaration/document/index.htm, 20 December 2005. German translation: Wolfgang Lautemann et al. (ed.), Geschichte in Quellen, *vol. 4, BSV, München, 1981, p. 90.*

23 **a** Match the following summaries A–C to the first three extracts from the Declaration of Independence in S 14:

A *This part is a list of things the American colonists believed the King of England had done wrong, and which justified their fight for independence.*

B *This part explains the purpose[4] of the document.*

C *This part describes individual rights and the relation between people and their governments ("theory of good government").*

b Write down your own summary of the last extract in S 14.

24 Write down the text of parts 3 and 4 (S 14) in German. Do not try to translate word-for-word, but instead concentrate on the meaning.

25 In your own words:

a Explain what the purpose of the Declaration of Independence was.

b List the rights each person has by nature. Explain what the terms exactly mean.

c Describe the relation between people and government.

d Explain what a "good government" is (see Task 23).

e Discuss why, according to the explanation of what a good government is, the list of grievances[5] in part 3 of the Declaration justified the separation from Great Britain.

26 Identify the democratic principles named in the Declaration of Independence that all democratic governments are founded on.

27 Making connections: Explain France's possible motives for supporting the American "rebels".

28 **Extra research:** Give a presentation on Thomas Jefferson, the man who was mainly responsible for writing the Declaration of Independence.

1 tyranny *Tyrannei, Gewaltherrschaft*
2 abolish sth. *etwas abschaffen, beseitigen*
3 consent *Zustimmung*
4 purpose *Zweck*
5 list of grievances *Beschwerdeliste, Klageliste*

Analysing political cartoons

A political cartoon shows a cartoonist's point of view on a topic[1] or issue[2]. However, it is often not easy to identify his or her point of view, especially if the cartoon was produced many years ago. In order to "get it", you need background information from classroom discussion, a textbook or your own research. Once you have a general idea of the topic, you can start to decode[3] the message the cartoonist is trying to convey[4]. Just as writers use a language with 26 letters from A to Z, political cartoonists use their own language, i.e. cartoon techniques that convey their points of view, for example symbols and visual analogies[5]. Symbols, as used in cartoons, represent larger ideas or issues. In analogies two things are compared visually or in writing in order to stress their similarities.

Study skills

Context: Identify the event the cartoon refers to. Look at the caption[6] to see where and when the cartoon was published and what type of magazine, newspaper or other publication it was in. Who was the intended audience for the cartoon?

Content: Describe the action taking place in the cartoon. Pay close attention to any captions, titles, labels[7], name tags, dialogue, or speech bubbles, as well as symbols used by the cartoonist to portray people, events and issues.

Target[8]**:** Who or what is being criticised? Is the cartoon criticising or sympathising with a person, group or country? On whose "side" is the cartoonist?

Technique: What techniques is the cartoonist using to express his or her view?

a Look for anything that seems exaggerated[9]. A cartoonist often exaggerates the characteristics of people's faces and clothes. Decide what point the cartoonist was trying to make through exaggeration.

b Look for symbols. Cartoonists use pictures as symbols for larger ideas, people, organizations, and so on.

c Look for analogies. Cartoonists describe a situation or event by comparing it to another historical, fictional or everyday situation or event. What two situations does the cartoon compare? What parallels does it draw?

Message: What is the cartoonist's message or comment? What is the cartoonist's position on the event? What is his or her point of view on the topic portrayed in the cartoon? Give examples to support your interpretation. What special groups would agree/disagree with the cartoon's messsage? Why? Do you agree with the cartoonist's message? Explain.

Evaluating[10] **cartoons as historical sources:** For historians, all sources are "windows to past events". What do we see and learn "through" the cartoon?

Activate your English

Talking about cartoons

Context:

- *The cartoon was published in ... by ...*
- *The cartoon refers to ...*
- *The characters represent / stand for / symbolize ...*
- *The caption is ironic/humorous/... because ...*

Techniques and points of view:

- *The animal is drawn / presented in a realistic / an unrealistic way.*
- *Their sizes are exaggerated to suggest to / show the reader that ...*
- *The character is portrayed favourably / unfavourably / as being ...*
- *in the background / in the foreground*
- *on the left / in the middle / in the centre / on the right*
- *at the top / at the bottom*
- *in the top right-hand corner / in the bottom left-hand corner*

Target and message:

- *The cartoonist wants to show / criticizes / makes fun of / tries to convince*[11] *people that ...*

1 topic *Thema*
2 issue *Problem, Angelegenheit, Streitpunkt*
3 decode sth. *etwas entschlüsseln*
4 convey (a message) *(eine Botschaft) vermitteln*
5 analogy *comparison between things which have similar features (= vergleichbare Merkmale), often used to help explain a principle or idea*
6 caption *words printed below a picture or cartoon*
7 label *Beschriftung*
8 target *Ziel(-richtung)*
9 exaggerate *übertreiben*
10 evaluate sth. *etwas einschätzen, beurteilen*
11 convince *überzeugen*

S 15 **"The Horse 'America', Throwing His Master", artist unknown, British cartoon, 1 August 1779**

Describing the action

A well-fed horse called "America" is throwing the rider out of the saddle, while a soldier, who is carrying a flag with 13 stars, is running towards the rider. The rider is wearing fine clothes, a wig[1] and a sash[2]; a medal[3] is pinned on his chest[4]. He is about to lose control of the horse: he has already lost his reins[5], but he has not actually fallen off yet, and his foot is still loosely in the stirrup[6]. He is not looking at the horse or at the soldier, but upward into space. His riding stick[7] is a cruel[8] instrument with weapons attached, which he has used to discipline the horse.

29 Identify where and when the cartoon was published.

30 **a** Identify the figures in the cartoon.

b Identify who or what is being criticized. (Tip: Who was "master" of "America" at the time when the cartoon was published? See the timeline, pp. 11–12, and the text, p. 14.)

31 Identify the symbols and explain what they stand for.

32 Identify the two situations which are compared (visual analogies). Complete the sentences:

A *The cartoon compares riding "the horse America" to …*

B *The cartoon shows a rider who is "not in the saddle" anymore. This can be compared to …*

33 Identify the event which the cartoon refers to.

34 Discuss the cartoonist's message.

35 Write a complete and detailed analysis of the cartoon.

1 wig *Perücke*
2 sash *Schärpe*
3 medal *Orden, Ehrenzeichen*
4 chest *Brust(korb)*
5 reins *Zügel*
6 stirrup *Steigbügel*
7 riding stick *Reitgerte*
8 cruel *grausam*

6 "A more perfect union" – Constitution[1] and government

"We the people"

When the Revolutionary War was over and the United States of America was finally independent from Britain, Americans began to govern themselves. However, the form of government was still unclear.

In 1787, after much debate and compromise[2], the US Constitution* was adopted[3]. It begins with the words "We the people of the United States, in order to form a more perfect union, establish[4] ..." and has been in force[5] until today.

The document outlines[6] the relationships between the people and their governments. The Constitution of 1787

- makes the people, and not a king, sovereign[7];
- declares that governments must be elected by the majority of the people;
- separates the powers* of the government into three branches that check and balance each other (see S 18).

A constitution in process

The Bill of Rights[8]* (see S 19) were added to the Constitution in 1791. Yet, slavery and the slave trade* continued to exist, especially in the southern states where slaves worked on the tobacco, rice and cotton plantations of their white owners (see p. 7). Only at the end of the long Civil War between the northern and southern states (1861–1865) was slavery abolished with the 13th Amendment (or addition).

Originally only white men with some property had the right to vote. Former male black slaves were given it in 1870 (15th Amendment); women did not win the right to vote until 1920 (19th Amendment).

S 16 **"Confidence in the constitution", US print, late 18th century**

Biography

George Washington
was the first president of the United States. Born in Virginia in 1732, he was trained as a surveyor[9], fought in the French and Indian War (1756–1763) in the Virginia militia, managed his plantation, Mount Vernon, and was active in Virginia politics before he was appointed[10] to command the Continental Army against the British in 1775. In 1781 he led the Continental Army to victory against British troops near Yorktown. In 1787 he presided[11] over the Constitutional Convention in Philadelphia, Pennsylvania, where the US Constitution was written. He was elected President of the new republic in 1789 and again in1792. In 1799, Washington died in Mount Vernon, Virginia.

1 constitution *basic law of a country (Verfassung)*
2 compromise *Kompromiss (Übereinkunft durch gegenseitige Zugeständnisse)*
3 adopt (a constitution) *(eine Verfassung) annehmen, verabschieden*
4 establish *errichten, verordnen*
5 be in force *in Kraft sein*
6 outline *umreißen, grob beschreiben*
7 sovereign *a nation's ruler (Souverän)*
8 Bill of Rights *Grundrechtekatalog*
9 surveyor *Landvermesser*
10 appoint sb. *jdn. ernennen*
11 preside *Vorsitz führen*

S 17 The US Constitution

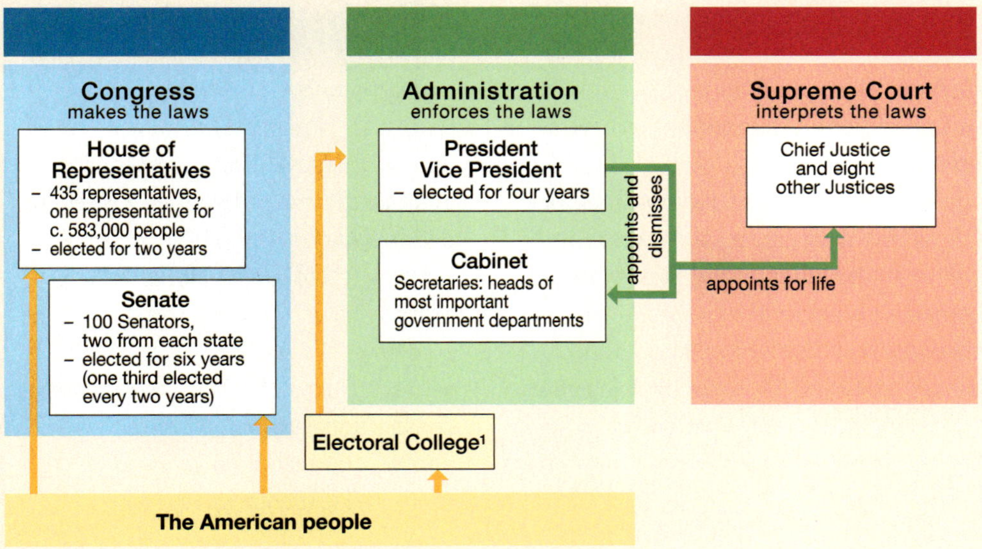

S 18 The system of "checks and balances" in the US Constitution

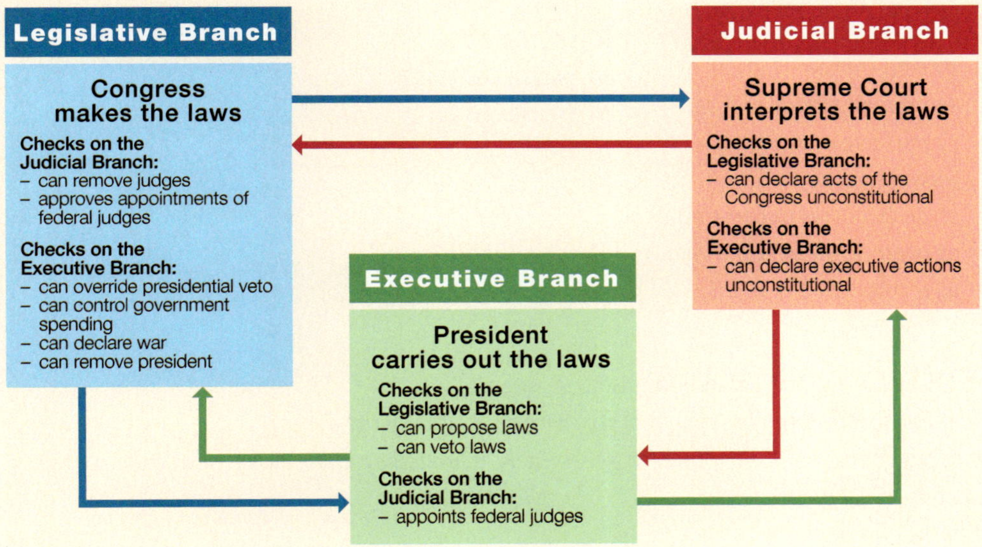

S 19 Guarantees of the US Bill of Rights, 1791

Freedom of religion	
Freedom of the press	
Freedom of speech	
Freedom of assembly[2]	gives citizens[3] the right to organize and to join any club, organization and party they wish; they are also free to hold public meetings.
Freedom and security of citizens	protects citizens against a search of their homes and arrest without a warrant[4].
Freedom of petition	gives citizens the right to contact their government representatives and ask them to work to pass a law or to change laws they do not like.
Right to a trial by jury[5]	is the right to a speedy and public trial[6] and a lawyer[7].

1 Electoral College *Wahlmänner*
2 freedom of assembly *Vereinigungsrecht*
3 citizen *inhabitant of a town, city or country (Bürger/Bürgerin)*
4 warrant *richterliche Anordnung, Haftbefehl*
5 trial by jury *Verhandlung vor einem Geschworenengericht*
6 trial *Prozess, Gerichtsverfahren*
7 lawyer *Rechtsanwalt*

36 **a** Read the text on p. 18 and create your own timeline titled "A constitution in progress". Write the dates below the line and the events, with explanations, above the line.
b Comment on your findings.

37 Give reasons why it is important to have a written constitution.

38 **Extra research:** Find a map of Washington, DC (guidebooks, Internet) and locate the government buildings of the three branches of American government (S 17).

39 To explain the US system of "checks and balances", copy and fill in the following chart. For help and further information, see S 18.

Activate your English

Talking about a constitution

appoint sb. / appointment *jdn. ernennen / Ernennung*
dismiss sb. *jdn. entlassen*
remove (judges) *(Richter) abberufen*
approve sth. *etw. genehmigen, billigen*
declare (war) *(Krieg) erklären*
override (a veto) *(ein Veto) aufheben*
propose (laws) *(Gesetze) vorschlagen, einbringen*
veto sth. *Einspruch gegen etw. einlegen*
constitutional *verfassungsgemäß*
unconstitutional *verfassungswidrig*
government spending *(Regierungs-)Ausgaben*

*The **power** ...*	*Which **branch** has the power?*	*Who **checks** the branch's power? (Can be more than one)*
1 to create and pass laws		
2 to veto laws		
3 to appoint federal judges		
4 to approve presidential appointments		
5 to declare laws unconstitutional		
6 to override presidential vetoes		
7 to remove the President		

40 The US Constitution is based on four principles:
1. *Popular sovereignty*: the power of government is held by the people.*
2. *Limited government: the power of government is limited by law / by the Constitution.*
3. *Separation of powers: ...*
4. *Checks and balances: ...*

Copy the US constitutional principles and add the explanations that are missing (for help see S 17, S 18).

41 After completing Task 40, split up into groups and create a poster for each of the four principles of the US Constitution. Each poster should include:
a the name of the principle, printed clearly;
b an explanation of what the principle means, including how it works in the government or how it is a part of the government;
c a drawing, picture or chart that reflects the idea of this principle.
Be prepared to explain your poster to the class.

42 Copy the first three rights of the Bill of Rights from S 19 and add the missing explanations.

43 Why did the US Congress add the Bill of Rights just four years after passing the Constitution? Tip: Compare and contrast the Declaration of Independence (see pp. 14–15, S 14) and the Constitution (S 17, S 18).

44 Discuss whether the government of the United States (S 17–S 19) is a "good government". For the idea of "good government", see the Declaration of Independence (see pp. 14–15, S 14, and Task 25 d).

The American Revolution

Key events

1607	First British colony in North America (Jamestown)
1756–1763	French and Indian War (= Seven Years' War)
1765	Stamp Act
1773	Boston Tea Party
1775–1783	War of Independence
1776	Declaration of Independence/ Bill of Rights
1783	Treaty of Paris

Key terms

Native Americans (= Indians), Pilgrim Fathers, Puritans, slave trade, colony, indentured servants, slavery, resistance, constitution, popular sovereignty, Bill of Rights, separation of powers, checks and balances

Key personalities

Thomas Jefferson
George Washington

History skills

Evaluating sources *(pp. 8–9)*
Analysing political cartoons *(pp. 16–17)*

Activate your English

Agreeing or disagreeing *(p. 6)*
Talking about statistics *(p. 7)*
Talking about cartoons *(p. 16)*
Talking about a constitution *(p. 20)*

S 20 **Donald Reilly, cartoon in *The New Yorker*, 2 January 1971, "We're here to escape religious persecution. What are you here for?"**

1 Discuss if more key events and key terms are needed to describe "The winning of independence" and "Creating a democracy" in America.
2 With the help of key events, key terms and key personalities, prepare a three-minute talk on:
  a "The winning of independence" in America,
  b "Creating a democracy" in America.
3 List the words and phrases you would use to describe
  a the elements of a cartoon and the terms and phrases needed to analyse it;
  b how people "resist" and the effects of their resistance.
4 In groups of three or four, organize the new vocabulary in two mind maps (see Appendix). Explain the connection between the words in your mind map and the chapter topic.
5 Create a crossword puzzle with the new vocabulary. Use synonyms, sentences with a missing word, translations, etc. for the clues in your crossword. For example: *Inhabitant of a town, city or country = CITIZEN.*
6 1763: The turning point in American colonial history? Explain the answer to the person sitting next to you. Does the person agree with your interpretation?
7 a Split up into groups of three: Study the cartoon in S 20, identify the event the cartoon is referring to and explain the caption. Formulate the answer of the little boy with the feathers on his head.
  b Compare your results.

Alex Haley, Roots, 1977
The novel tells the story of the ancestors of African-American writer Alex Haley. The story goes back to the time of slavery in the southern United States and even to the West African roots of Haley's family in the 18th century.

Glossary of terms

balance of power: the theory in politics that the best way of keeping international peace is to distribute power among states equally. The aim is that no state should achieve a dominant position. In the 18th and 19th centuries Britain actively promoted the "balance of power" on the European continent.

Bill of Rights: the ten amendments (or additions) added to the Constitution of the United States → in 1791 which guarantee certain freedoms (religious and political freedom, the right to bear arms, the right to life, liberty and property, protection in criminal trials, etc.).

checks and balances: see p. 19.

colony: A country or area that is ruled by another, more powerful, country. In former times the local native population of a colony did not enjoy full rights. Many were forced into slave labour or driven out of their homes. Their land was sometimes taken and given to settlers from the ruling country. Foreign customs, religions or legal systems were imposed.

constitution: a country's highest law upon which all other laws are based. It is the basis for government because it states how the government will be organized. It describes how the government is formed, who makes it up, and how laws are passed and amended. A constitution also defines the limits of the power of the government. In Germany the constitution, called the *Grundgesetz* (Basic Law), includes a catalogue of citizens' basic rights.

indentured servant: in former times, a person who signed a contract to work for an employer in another country. The employer then paid for that person's passage to the new country. During the 17th century, most of the white workers in Maryland and Virginia came from England as indentured servants. They sold themselves to an agent or ship captain before leaving Britain who then sold them to a buyer in the colonies →. Most indentured servants in the colonies were young, single males in their teens or twenties. They typically worked for somebody for seven years; in most cases as household servants or unskilled workers on farms and plantations. In theory, the person only sold his or her labour. In practice, however, indentured servants were basically slaves. The treatment of the servant was harsh and often brutal. The system developed because of the labour shortage in the colonies. The tobacco plantations in Virginia needed a lot of workers. The local Indian population was unwilling to work there, so the plantation owners "bought" poor English adults who were slowly replaced by African slaves (slavery, slave trade →).

Native American: a member of any of the races of the original people living in America (before the arrival of European settlers). Originally referred to as Indians by European settlers.

Pilgrim Fathers: a group of English Protestants who wanted to completely separate from the Church of England. They thus emigrated to North America in 1620 and founded Plymouth Colony in the area now known as Cape Cod Bay, Massachussetts. (Puritans →)

popular sovereignty: the power that the people of a country have to govern themselves or another country.

Puritans: a group of English Protestants who wanted to reform (or "purify") the Church of England during the Protestant Reformation. In the 1630s, several thousand Puritans came from England to the Massachusetts Bay Colony north of Plymouth Colony (Pilgrim Fathers →) and founded Boston. Between 1629 and 1640, altogether about 21,000 English colonists (Puritans and Pilgrims) crossed the Atlantic Ocean to settle in New England. The values of these settlers strongly influenced the culture of the American colonies and later of the United States.

resistance: the refusal to accept a political, economic or social change or to follow instructions or laws. Resistance can take many different forms.

separation of powers: the principle of modern constitutions (e.g. the US Constitution) that the political power of the government is divided between the executive branch (e.g. the US president), the legislative branch (e.g. US Congress) and the judicial branch (e.g. the US Supreme Court).

slavery: the state or practice in which a person is legally or illegally owned by another and is forced to work for them. Slavery has existed for thousands of years. The winners in a battle often enslaved the losers instead of killing them. The first slave auction in the American colonies was held in Jamestown, Virginia, in 1638. Although slavery is illegal today, it still exists. Millions of people worldwide are enslaved or work as forced labourers.

slave trade: the business of capturing people and buying and selling them as enslaved workers. Ten to twelve million African slaves were bought to work on plantations and in mines in the Americas between 1450 and the end of the 19th century. The majority was shipped to Brazil, the Caribbean, and the Spanish Empire. Less than five per cent travelled to North America. This happened with the full and active cooperation of African kings and merchants who captured them inland and brought them to the coast. It has been estimated that many slaves died before even reaching the coast and the ships of the Portuguese, Dutch and British slave traders. Conditions on the slave ships were terrible. But although the death rate was about 13 per cent, the trade was still enormously profitable. As a result of the slave trade, five times as many Africans arrived in the Americas as did Europeans. It has been calculated that the population in Africa in the mid 19th century would have been twice as high if the slave trade had not happened.

Glossary of persons

Bradford, William (1590–1657) One of the leaders of the Pilgrim Fathers →, who settled in Plymouth Bay. He was elected Governor of Plymouth Colony in 1621 and re-elected 30 times. He kept a journal of the history of the first 30 years of the Plymouth Colony. He worked to keep peace with Native Amricans. *p. 6*

Chodowiecki, Daniel (1726–1801) German-Polish painter and the most famous engraver of his time. His works include several thousand drawings, paintings and engravings, mostly published in popular calendars and almanacs. *p. 12*

Columbus, Christopher (c. 1451–1506) Italian navigator and explorer in the service of Spain. He discovered the New World in 1492. *p. 4*

George III (1738–1820) King of Great Britain and Ireland, 1760–1820, and of Hanover, 1815–1820. During his reign the American colonies → were lost. Great Britain and Ireland were joined together to form the United Kingdom. He became insane in 1811 and his son acted as regent for the rest of his reign. *pp. 11–13*

Jefferson, Thomas (1743–1826) See Biography, *p. 14*

Oertel, Johannes A. S. (1823–1909) German/American painter. Born in Nuremberg, Germany, he emigrated to the USA in 1848. *p. 13*

Paine, Thomas (1737–1809) Born in England, he emigrated to America in 1774. He became involved in politics in the American colonies → and published the enormously successful pamphlet *Common Sense* (January 1776), in which he argued that the colonies should be given independence. *p. 12*

Steuben, Friedrich von (1730–1794) German officer. He fought on the American side in the American War of Independence. He helped to teach military discipline in the Continental Army through his drilling techniques. He died in Steubenville, N.Y. To honour von Steuben parades are held in New York, Chicago and Philadelphia during the month of September. *p. 14*

Washington, George (1732–1799) See Biography, *p. 18.*

Charts and diagrams

Mind map

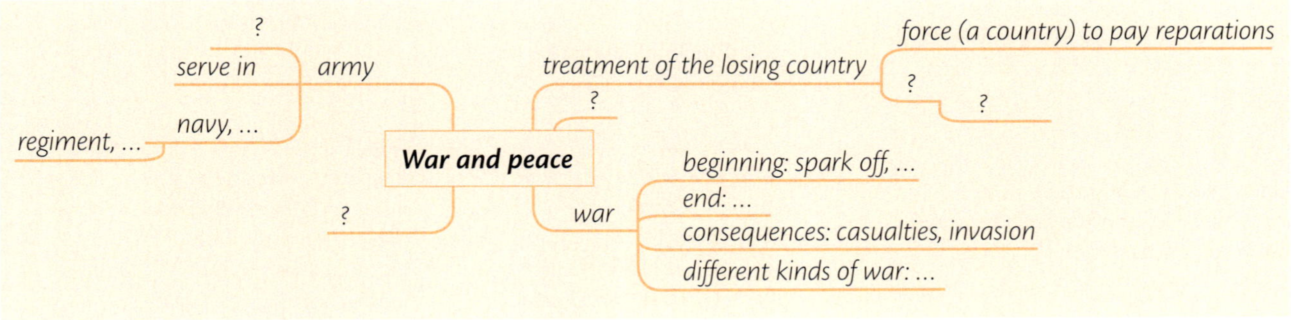

Event map

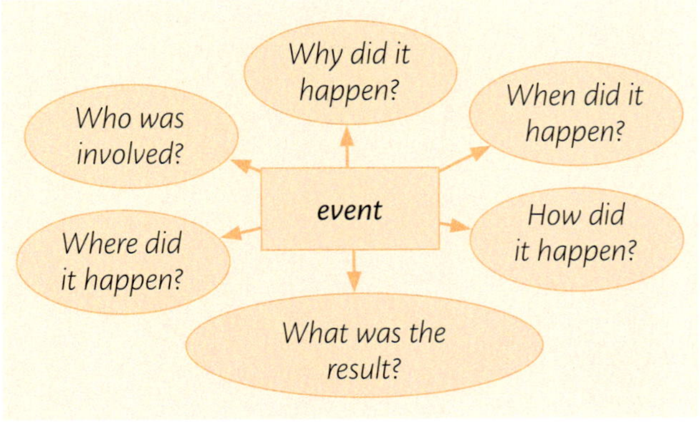

English-German vocabulary

A

abdication *Abdankung*
abolish sth. *etwas abschaffen beseitigen*
abolition *Abschaffung, Auflösung*
accept sth. *etwas anerkennen, akzeptieren*
account *Bericht*
act *Gesetz*
adopt sth. *etwas annehmen, verabschieden*
adoption *Annahme, Verabschiedung*
agree with sth. / sb. *einer Sache / jdm. zustimmen*
agriculture *Landwirtschaft*
aim *Ziel, Absicht*
allow sth. *etwas erlauben*
analogy *Analogie, Entsprechung, Übereinstimmung*
ancestor *Vorfahr/in, Ahn/in*
anger *Wut, Zorn*
appoint sb. *jdn. ernennen*
appointment *Ernennung*
approve sth. *etwas genehmigen, billigen*
area *Gebiet*
assembly *Versammlung*
attend sth. [- '-] *etwas besuchen*
audience ['ɔ:diəns] *Adressaten*
authority *Autorität, Erlaubnis*

B

bear – bore – borne sth. *etwas ertragen*
bias ['baɪəs] *Tendenz, Voreingenommenheit, Neigung*
Bill of Rights *Grundrechtekatalog*
build-up *Aufbau*
bulleted list *Aufzählung (mit Aufzählungszeichen am Zeilenanfang)*

C

caption *Bildunter/überschrift*
capture sth./sb. ['kæptʃə] *etwas einnehmen, jdn. gefangen nehmen*
cartoon *Karikatur*
census *Volkszählung*
character *Charakter, Gesinnung*
cheer sb. *jdm. zujubeln*
cheerful *freundlich, heiter*
chest *Brust(korb)*
citizen ['sɪtɪzn] *Bürger*
colonization *Kolonisierung*
colony ['- - -] *Kolonie*
column ['kɒləm ☆ 'kɑ:ləm] *(Heeres-) Kolonne*
compare sth. *etwas vergleichen*
complain *sich beschweren*
complaint *Beschwerde*
compromise ['kɒmprəmaɪz ☆ 'kɑ:m-] *Kompromiss*
conclusion *Schlussfolgerung*
Congress ['- -] *Kongress*
connection *Verbindung*
consent [kən'sent] *Zustimmung*
constitution *Verfassung*
constitutional *verfassungsgemäß*
context *Kontext, Zusammenhang*
contract ['- -] *(geschäftlicher) Vertrag*
contrast sth. [kən'trɑ:st ☆ -'træst] *etwas gegenüberstellen*
convey sth. *etwas vermitteln*
convince sb. *jdn. überzeugen*
cotton *Baumwolle*
criticize sb. *jdn. kritisieren*
crop(s) *Feldfrucht; Ernte*
crop failures *Ernteausfälle*
crowd *Menge*
cruel ['kru:əl] *grausam*
customs *Sitten, Zoll*
customs officer *Zollbeamter/in, Zöllner/in, Mautner/in*

D

decent ['di:snt] *anständig, annehmbar*
declaration [ˌdeklə'reɪʃn] *Erklärung*
Declaration of Independence [ˌdeklə'reɪʃn] *Unabhängigkeitserklärung*
declare sth. *etwas erklären*
decode sth. *etwas entschlüsseln*
decrease *sinken, zurückgehen; Sinken, Rückgang, Abnahme*
defeat *Niederlage*
defeat sb./sth. *jdn./etwas besiegen, schlagen; etwas ablehnen*
delegate ['delɪgət] *Abgeordneter, Beauftragter*
democracy [di'mɒkrəsi ☆ -'mɑ:k-] *Demokratie*
disagree *ablehnen*
disappear *verschwinden*
disease [dɪ'zi:z] *Krankheit*
dismiss sb. *jdn. entlassen*
dismissal *Entlassung*
disobedience [ˌdɪsə'bi:diəns] *Ungehorsam*
dissolve [dɪ'zɒlv ☆ -'zɑ:lv] *auflösen*
draw conclusions *Schlüsse ziehen*
drop *Rückgang*

E

earn sth. [ɜ:n] *etwas verdienen*
empire *Kaiserreich, Weltreich*
endure sth. *etwas ertragen*
engraving *Stich, Druckgrafik*
establish sth. *etwas einrichten, errichten, verordnen*
estimate ['estɪmeɪt] *schätzen*
evaluate sth. *etwas einschätzen, beurteilen*
event map *Ereignisdiagramm*
evidence *Beleg, Beweis*
exaggerate (sth.) [ɪg'zædʒəreɪt] *(etwas) übertreiben*
excerpt ['eksɜ:pt] *Auszug, Ausschnitt*
exclude sb. *jdn. ausschließen*
exclusion *Ausschluss*
execution [ˌeksɪ'kju:ʃn] *Hinrichtung*
Executive Branch [ɪg'zekjətɪv] *Exekutive*
exhibition [ˌ- - '- -] *Ausstellung*
exhibit [- '- -] *Ausstellungsstück*

F

favourable *günstig, vorteilhaft*
fear *Angst*
fertile ['fɜ:taɪl ☆ 'fɜ:rtl] *fruchtbar*
force *Kraft, Armee*
foreground *Vordergrund*
found sth. *etwas gründen*
freedom of assembly *Vereinigungsrecht*
French Indian War *Siebenjähriger Krieg*
further sth. *etwas vorantreiben, fördern*

G

general *allgemein*
go up *heraufgehen*
goods *Güter*
government spending *Regierungsausgaben*
gradual ['grædʒuəl] *allmählich, langsam*
grievance *Beschwerde, Klage*

H

have a say *Mitspracherechte haben*
have blind spots *„auf einem Auge blind sein"*
humorous ['hju:mərəs] *witzig, humorvoll*

I

illegal [- '- -] *ungesetzlich, illegal*
impose sth. etwas auferlegen
increase *(an)steigen, (an)wachsen; Anstieg*
independence *Unabhängigkeit*
indentured servant *Dienstverpflichteter/in*
indifference *Gleichgültigkeit*
industrial enterprise *Industrieunternehmen*
inferior *niedere*
inhabitant *Einwohner/in*
injustice [ɪn'dʒʌstɪs] *Ungerechtigkeit*
insurrection *Aufruhr, Aufstand, Erhebung*
introduce sb. / sth. *jdn. / etwas einführen*
investigation *Untersuchung*
involuntary [- '- - - -] *unfreiwillig*
ironic [aɪ'rɒnɪk ☆ -rɑ:n-] *ironisch*
issue ['ɪʃu:, BE also 'ɪsju:] *Problem, Angelegenheit, Streitpunkt*

J

Judicial Branch [dʒu'dɪʃl] *Jurisdiktion*
just *gerecht*

justice ['dʒʌstɪs] *Gerechtigkeit*
justify sth. *etwas rechtfertigen*

L

label ['leɪbl] *Beschriftung*
label sth. ['leɪbl] *etwas beschriften, kennzeichnen*
labourer *Arbeitskraft, Arbeiter/in*
last *dauern*
law *Gesetz*
law-abiding ['lɔː əbaɪdɪŋ] *gesetzestreu*
lawyer ['lɔːjə] *Rechtsanwalt / -anwältin*
left-hand (corner) *linke (Ecke)*
Legislative Branch ['ledʒɪslətɪv ☆ -leɪtɪv] *Legislative*
liberty *Freiheit*
list of grievances *Beschwerdeliste, Klageliste*

M

manner *way*
medal ['medəl] *Orden, Ehrenzeichen*
member *Mitglied*
memoir ['memwɑː] *Lebenserinnerung*
memorial *Denkmal*
merchant *Kaufmann / Kauffrau*
militia [mə'lɪʃə] *Bürgerwehr, Miliz*

N

Native American *Ureinwohner Amerikas, Indianer/in*

O

object to sth. [əb'dʒekt] *etwas einwenden*
opinion *Meinung*
outline sth. *etwas umreißen, grob beschreiben*
overcome sth. *etwas überwinden*
override sth. *etwas aufheben*
overthrow *Umsturz (einer Regierung)*
own sth. *etwas besitzen*
owner *Besitzer/in*

P

painting *Gemälde*
pamphlet *Broschüre, Prospekt, Streitschrift*
pass a law *ein Gesetz verabschieden*
pedestal *Sockel, Unterbau*
Pilgrim Fathers *Pilgerväter*
plantation *Plantage*
point of view *Standpunkt*
poised *bereit*
popular sovereignty *Volkssouveränität*
preside *Vorsitz führen*
primary source *Primärquelle*
prince *Prinz, Fürst*
principality *Fürstentum*
process sth. *etwas weiterverarbeiten*
property *Besitz*
propose sth. *etwas vorschlagen, einbringen*
protect sb. *jdn. schützen*
protection *Schutz*
publish sth. *etwas veröffentlichen*
purpose ['pɜːpəs] *Zweck, Absicht*

R

railway (BE) *Eisenbahn*
railway bridge *Eisenbahnbrücke*
railway net *Eisenbahnliniennetz*
raise sth. *etwas aufbringen*
recognize sth. *etwas (an)erkennen*
record *Aufzeichnung*
refer to sth. *sich beziehen auf etwas*
refusal [rɪ'fjuːzl] *Weigerung*
reliability [rɪˌlaɪə'bɪləti] *Glaubwürdigkeit, Zuverlässigkeit*
reliable [rɪ'laɪəbl] *verlässlich*
remain *bleiben*
remove sb. *jdn. abberufen*
reorganization *Umgestaltung*
repeal sth. *etwas aufheben, abschaffen*
representative *Abgeordneter/in*
require sth. *etwas (er)fordern*
resist sth. *etwas widerstehen*
resistance *Widerstand*
result *Ergebnis, Resultat*
result in sth. *in etwas münden, zu etwas führen*
riding stick *Reitgerte*
right-hand (corner) *rechte (Ecke)*
riot ['raɪət] *Aufruhr, Krawall*
rise *Anstieg*
rise by *um etwas (an)steigen*
rise in sth. *Anstieg in etwas*
root *Wurzeln*
rule *Regel; herrschen*

S

sash *Schärpe*
savage ['sævɪdʒ] *wild*
secondary source *Sekundärquelle, Sekundärtext*
servant *Diener/in*
serve as sth. *dienen als etwas*
serve sb. *jdm. dienen*
settlement *Abkommen, Übereinkunft; Besiedlung, Siedlung*
settler *Siedler/in*
Seven Years War *Siebenjähriger Krieg*
sharp *stark*
similar *gleich, vergleichbar*
slave *Sklave*
Slavery Abolition Act *Gesetz zur Abschaffung der Sklaverei*
slave trade *Sklavenhandel*
slavery *Sklaverei*
slight *langsam, leicht*
smash sth. *etwas zerschlagen*
source *Quelle*
sovereign ['sɒvrɪn ☆ 'sɑːvrən] *Souverän*
Stamp Act *Stempelgesetz*
steady *gleichmäßig, stetig*
stirrup *Steigbügel*
strength *Kraft*
stress sth. *etwas betonen*
suffer *leiden*
suffrage *Wahlrecht*
supply *Versorgung, Nachschub*
support sb. *jdn. / etwas unterstützen, belegen*
surveyor [sə'veɪə] *Landvermesser/in*

T

target *Ziel(-richtung)*
tax *Steuer*
therefore *deshalb, also*
threat [θret] *Drohung*
threaten sb. ['θretn] *jdn. bedrohen, jdm. drohen*
thus *so, somit, daher, folglich*
topic *Thema*
torment sb. *jdn. quälen*
trade *handeln; Handel, Gewerbe*
trading post *Handelsniederlassung, -station*
traitor *Verräter/in*
treasure ['treʒə] *Schatz*
treaty ['triːti] *Vertrag (zwischen Staaten)*
Treaty of Paris ['triːti] *Pariser Vertrag*
trial ['traɪəl] *Prozess, Gerichtsverfahren*
trial by jury ['traɪəl] *Verhandlung vor einem Geschworenengericht*
tribe *Stamm*

U

unconstitutional *verfassungswidrig*
unfavourable *ungünstig, unvorteilhaft, negativ*
unification *Vereinigung*
unjust *ungerecht*

V

veto sth. ['viːtəʊ ☆ -toʊ] *Einspruch gegen etwas einlegen*
victory *Sieg*
view *Sicht*
vote *wählen; Wahl, Abstimmungsergebnis*
vote on sth. *über etwas abstimmen*

W

warrant *richterliche Anordnung, Haftbefehl*
wig *Perücke*

Y

yet *jedoch, aber*

Historical dictionary

(Analysing, discussing and arguing)

A

Abgaben dues *(Pl.)*
Abkommen agreement, settlement
etwas ablehnen disagree with sth., reject sth.
Abnahme decrease
etwas abschaffen abolish sth., repeal sth.
Abschaffung abolition, repeal
Absicht aim, intention
absichtlich deliberate
über etwas abstimmen vote on sth.
jdn. abwählen vote sb. out
allgemein general, universal
allmählich gradual
also therefore
etwas anerkennen recognize sth.
Angaben data, information
etwas angeben indicate sth.
angeklagt sein go on trial for sth.
Angelegenheit matter, issue
zum Angriff übergehen launch an attack
Anlass geben zu etwas give rise to sth.
Anspruch claim
um etwas ansteigen rise by sth. *(eine Zahl oder eine Menge)*
Anstieg increase, rise
etwas anstreben aspire to sth.
(prozentualer) Anteil percentage
Anteil an etwas proportion of sth.
Armee army, force
Armenhilfe poor relief
Aufbau build-up
etwas auferlegen impose sth.
etwas aufheben (außer Kraft setzen) overrule, override sth.; *(widerrufen)* abolish sth.
auflösen dissolve
Aufstand revolt, insurrection
jdn. ausbeuten exploit sb.
Auseinandersetzung dispute
Ausfuhr export
Ausmaß extent
Auswanderung emigration
Auswirkung auf etwas effect on sth.

B

Baumwolle cotton
beachtenswert remarkable
bedeutend notable, significant
jdn. bedrohen, jdm. drohen threaten sb.
Bedrohung threat, menace
Bedürfniss need
etwas begrüßen welcome, greet sth.
etwas behaupten claim sth.
etwas beitragen contribute sth.
etwas bekommen get, gain sth.
jdn. beleidigen insult sb.
Beschwerde grievance
jdn. benachteiligen discriminate against sb.
Bericht account; report
etwas besetzen occupy sth.
etwas besitzen own sth.
etwas beschränken limit sth.
jdn. beschuldigen accuse sb.
sich beschweren complain
Besiedlung settlement
Besitz property
Besitzer/in owner
bestehen aus sth. consist of sth.
etwas bestimmen determine sth.
an etwas beteiligt involved in sth.
etwas betonen emphasize sth., stress sth.
Betrachter/in viewer
jdn. vor etwas bewahren keep sb. from sth
Beweis evidence
sich auf etwas beziehen refer to sth.
Bürgerrechte civil rights

D

daher thus
dauern last
Denkmal memorial
deshalb therefore
deutlich noticeably
dienen als etwas serve as sth.
jdm. dienen serve sb.
Diener/in servant

E

Eindruck impression
einflussreich influential
eingreifen intervene
einmarschieren (in etwas) invade (sth.)
etwas einrichten establish sth.
Einspruch gegen etwas einlegen veto sth.
Eisenbahn railway (BE) = (AE) railroad
Einwanderung immigration
Einwohner/in inhabitant
entstehen arise
Entwicklung development
Ergebnis outcome, result
jdn. ernennen appoint sb.
Ernte crops
Ernteausfall crop failure
etwas erobern conquer sth.
Errungenschaft achievement
jdn. erschießen shoot sb. dead
etwas ertragen endure sth.
Erwerb acquisition
Exekutive Executive Branch

F

Feind enemy
Feindschaft hostility
feindselig hostile
flüchten flee
Folge consequence
folglich thus
jdn. foltern torture sb.
etwas fördern further sth., promote sth.
Forderung demand
Forderungen stellen present demands
Freiheit liberty
Friedenskonferenz peace conference
Friedensvereinbarung peace settlement
etwas führen conduct sth.
zu etwas führen give rise to sth., result in sth.

G

Gebiet area
jdn. gefangen nehmen capture sb.
im Gegensatz zu jdm. / etwas in contrast to / with sb. / sth.
gerecht just
Gerechtigkeit justice
jdn. wegen etwas vor Gericht stellen try sb. (in court) for sth.
Gerichtsverfahren trial
Gesellschaft society
Gesetz act, law
ein Gesetz verabschieden pass a law
gesetzestreu law-abiding
Gewaltenteilung separation of powers
gewöhnlich ordinary
gleich equal
Gleichheit equality
etwas gründen found sth.
günstig favourable
Güter goods

H

Handel commerce, trade
mit / in etwas handeln deal / trade with / in sth.
Haupt-, chief, principal
hauptsächlich (Adj) main, principal; *(Adv)* mainly, principally, especially
jdn. herausfordern challenge sb.
Herrschaft reign
herrschen rule
etwas hervorbringen bring about sth.
etwas hervorrufen provoke sth.
Hinrichtung execution
Höhepunkt zenith, peak

I

an jdm. / etwas interessiert interested in sb. / sth
ironisch ironic

J

jedoch yet, however
Jurisdiktion Judicial Branch

K

Kampf um etwas struggle for sth.
Karikatur cartoon
kaum hardly
Kolonie colony
Kolonisierung colonization
Kompromiss compromise
jdm. den Krieg erklären declare war on sb.
jdn. kritisieren criticize sb.
kurzfristig short-term

L

Land territory
langfristig long-term
Last burden, load
Legislative Legislative Branch
leiden suffer
etwas leiten direct sth.
jdn. / etwas loben praise sb. / sth.
etwas lösen resolve sth.

M

Mangel an etwas lack of sth.
Massenvernichtungswaffen weapons of mass destruction
Mehrheitsbeschluss majority decision
Meinung opinion
Menge crowd
Menschenrechte human rights
etwas missachten violate sth.
Mitgliedschaft membership
Mitspracherechte haben have a say

N

Niedergang decline
Niederlage defeat
Nutzen ziehen aus etwas benefit from sth.

P

Partei party
Pilgerväter Pilgrim Fathers
plötzlich sudden
von jdm. / etwas profitieren profit from sb. / sth.

Q

Quelle source

R

Rache revenge
Reagieren auf etwas respond to sth.
etwas rechtfertigen justify sth.
Rechtsanwalt/-wältin lawyer, solicitor
Regel rule
reichlich plentiful
Resultat result, outcome
Revolution revolution
Rückgang decrease, drop
Rückschlag setback

S

jdm. / etwas schaden harm sb., damage sth.
etwas schätzen estimate sth.
scheitern fail
Schlacht battle
Schlüsse ziehen draw conclusions
Schutz protection
jdn. schützen protect sb.
Segelschiff sailing ship
Sekundärtext secondary source
Sicht view
Sichtweise perspective
Siedler/in settler
Sieg victory
sinken decrease
Sklave slave
Sklaverei slavery
somit thus
Staatenbund federation
Staatshaushalt state budget
Stamm tribe
Standpunkt point of view
stark sharp
steigen increase
Steuer tax
Stolz auf etwas pride in sth.

T

Territorium territory
Thema topic
mit etwas zu tun haben deal with sth.

U

Überlegenheit superiority
etwas übertreiben exaggerate sth.
jdn. überzeugen convince sb.; persuade sb.
Umstand circumstance
Unabhängigkeit independence
unfreiwillig involuntary
ungerecht unjust
Ungerechtigkeit injustice
ungesetzlich illegal
ungünstig unfavourable
sich unterscheiden von / in etwas differ from / in sth.
jdn. / etwas unterstützen support sb.
Untersuchung investigation
etwas unterzeichnen sign sth.
unzufrieden mit etwas dissatisfied with sth.
Ursache cause

V

etwas verabschieden pass sth. *(z. B. ein Gesetz)*; adopt sth. *(z. B. einen Haushalt)*
Verbesserung improvement
etwas verbieten outlaw sth.
etwas vereinigen join sth. together
Vereinigung unification
Verfassung constitution
verfassungsgemäß constitutional
verfassungswidrig unconstitutional
vergleichbar similar
im Verhältnis zu etwas in proportion to sth.
etwas verhandeln negotiate sth.
etwas verhindern prevent sth.
etwas veröffentlichen publish sth.
Versammlung assembly
versäumen, etwas zu tun fail to do sth.
(geschäftlicher) Vertrag contract
Vertrag (zwischen Staaten) treaty
jdn. verurteilen sentence sb.
Volkssouveränität popular sovereignty
etwas voranbringen advance sth.
Vorherrschaft dominance, hegemony
etwas vorschlagen propose sth.

W

Waffenruhe ceasefire
Waffenstillstand armistice
Wahl vote, election
wählbar eligible
jdn. / etwas wählen vote for sb. / sth.
Wahlrecht suffrage
Weigerung refusal
sich wenden gegen jdn. / etwas oppose sb. / sth.
Widerstand resistance
etwas wiederherstellen restore sth.

Z

etwas zeigen point sth. out
Zeitalter age
Zeitpunkt moment
Zeitspanne period of time
Ziel aim

Ziel(-richtung) target
jdm. zujubeln cheer sb.
etwas zurückweisen reject sth.
einer Sache / jdm. zustimmen agree with sth. / sb.
Zustimmung agreement, consent
Zweck purpose
jdn. zwingen force, compel sb.

Abbreviations and symbols

AE	(mainly or exclusively) American English
BE	(mainly or exclusively) British English
e.g.	Lat. *exempli gratia* = for example
p., pp.	page, pages
sb.	somebody
sth.	something
☆	American pronunciation follows
→	see Appendix

Regular differences in American pronunciation – as for instance the [r] after vowels – have not been given.

Acknowledgements

akg-images: 11, 15, 16, 20 r.; bpk / Kunstbibliothek, SMB / Knud Petersen: 6; Massachusetts Historical Society, Boston: 13; The Cartoon Bank, New York: 23; ullstein – Granger Collection: 7, 9, 10, 14 / S11, S12, 19, 20 / S16

Nicht in allen Fällen war es uns möglich, die Rechteinhaber der Abbildungen ausfindig zu machen. Für eventuell entstandene Fehler oder Auslassungen bitten wir um Verständnis. Berechtigte Ansprüche werden selbstverständlich im Rahmen der üblichen Vereinbarungen abgegolten.